Contents

KU-549-603

>>> e-guidelines 4

e-learning in outreach

Glyn Owen and Khawar Iqbal

n iace

promoting adult learning

©2004 National Institute of Adult Continuing Education
(England and Wales)
21 De Montfort Street
Leicester
LE1 7GE

Company registration no. 2603322
Charity registration no. 1002775

NIACE has a broad remit to promote lifelong learning opportunities for adults. NIACE works to develop increased participation in education and training, particularly for those who do not have easy access because of class, gender, age, race, language and culture, learning difficulties or disabilities, or insufficient financial resources.

You can find NIACE online at www.niace.org.uk

Cataloguing in Publication Data
A CIP record of this title is available from the British Library

Designed and typeset by Patrick Armstrong Book Production Services, London

Printed and bound in the UK by Latimer Trend
ISBN: 1 86201 227 X

Acknowledgements

Many people have been involved in the production of this guide to good practice. They include over 300 Adult and Community Learning practitioners, managers and support workers.

People have contributed in a number of ways, but all have unhesitatingly given their time, ideas and support for the project. Thank you to everybody who: participated in on-line focus groups at the start of the writing process and shared their thoughts and experiences with peers; completed on-line questionnaires; gave one-to-one interviews describing their own practices for inclusion as case studies; shared ideas in workshops and group interviews at various stages in the book's development; reviewed early drafts and provided focused and constructive feedback, and in some cases their own materials for inclusion.

In particular, thanks must go to

> Anne Chester	Redcar Adult Learning Service
> John Collins	North Yorkshire County Council Community Education Service
> Richard Heath	Coventry Adult Education Service
> Kate Johnson	National Museums Liverpool
> Brenda Barnett	Leeds College of Technology
> Lynda Moorcroft	Buckinghamshire Adult Learning
> Phillip Vogel	I Can Do IT Project – Adult Community Learning – South Dartmoor
> Stuart Smith	Computing Bradford
> Diane Gardiner	North East Lincolnshire UK Online Project
> Penny Bryant	Rutland County Council

Also thanks to Sonia Best at NIACE, for her consistently good-humoured support and for lending her excellent organisational skills to the research and writing processes.

Special thanks to Angela Wood at NIACE for commissioning the research, her kind direction and positive assurance throughout the project, her willingness to use innovative research techniques along side more traditional methods, and for her editorial input.

Glyn Owen
Khawar Iqbal
August 2004

1

Introduction

E-learning is having an immense impact on all forms of education. The portable nature of laptops and associated equipment means that outreach workers can now benefit from access to a wealth of technology, information and learning resources. E-learning in particular can help increase learner participation, especially if it is linked with outreach activities, providing the ideal formula for integrating Information and Communication Technology (ICT) into adult learning in the community. The use of technology can offer an interactive and interesting learning experience, especially when used in the teaching of non-ICT-related subjects, where traditionally learners thought that ICT was 'not for them'.

In 2003–4, NIACE conducted research with providers of Adult and Community Learning (ACL) into the impact of e-learning on outreach activities. Over 300 adult education providers in the further education and ACL sectors informed this research by completing online questionnaires, participating in e-focus groups and workshops and allowing their activities to form the basis of case studies. The findings from this research have provided the background information for this guide.

This guide provides information, guidance and support for practitioners who wish to engage in e-learning in the community, whether they are already engaged in outreach or not. It covers all aspects of:

> teaching
> learning and the management of learning
> using technology in an outreach context

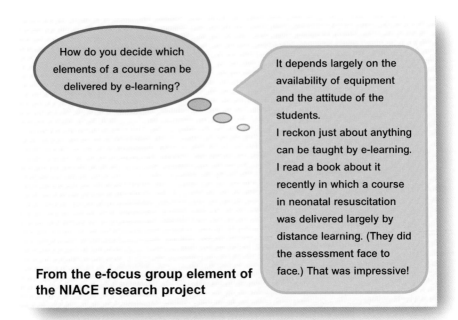

How do you decide which elements of a course can be delivered by e-learning?

It depends largely on the availability of equipment and the attitude of the students.
I reckon just about anything can be taught by e-learning. I read a book about it recently in which a course in neonatal resuscitation was delivered largely by distance learning. (They did the assessment face to face.) That was impressive!

From the e-focus group element of the NIACE research project

It aims to demonstrate that e-learning is a combination of processes and tools that can enhance the learning experience for adult learners in any curriculum area.

The guide is one of a series aimed at sharing effective practice among education practitioners. It was produced by NIACE in association with Yorkshire and Humber Development Consortium Ltd, who conducted the fieldwork.

Respondents to the NIACE online questionnaire cited the following reasons for using e-learning:

> it increases student participation,

> it encourages learners to go on to access further training in related and unrelated fields,

> it attracts more learners,

> it helps create a positive learning environment,

> it enhances teaching methods,

> it increases communication between staff and learners,

> it empowers learners,

> it helps learners improve their language and gain basic IT skills, and gives them more confidence,

> it encourages new links with different learning providers, community groups and networks,

> it gives access to learning without the need to travel long distances,

> it widens the range of teaching and learning methods,

> it helps learners back into the workplace,

> it provides increased motivation,

> it offers a wider range of materials,

> it is able to develop a much wider scope of provision,

> it offers transferable skills and tools to improve learners' quality of life and job opportunities.

Photo by Nick Hayes

2

So, what is outreach and e-learning?

Outreach

Talk to a dozen tutors who use ICT and they will each have their own views about outreach. For some people, outreach means travelling from one well-equipped learning centre with a broadband connection to another. For them 'outreach' really means 'travel', or working somewhere away from the main site. To another person it means carrying ten laptops in the boot of a car to a remote village hall, finding the caretaker to open up, checking that the heating is on, setting up an impromptu wireless network, making sure the extension power leads don't contravene Health and Safety rules, turning on the water boiler for tea, and then, and only then, welcoming the class.

There are, of course, many other types of outreach: the mobile ICT centre (with or without satellite) that trundles up and down the hills and dales of rural Britain, computers set up in local pubs and clubs that are visited by tutors on a regular basis, laptops at home schemes, and many more.

For the purpose of this guide, outreach means any teaching and learning situation that takes place away from the delivering organisation's main site.

e-learning

While most tutors may think they understand what is meant by 'outreach', e-learning is an area of potential confusion, and it has many definitions. NIACE believes that e-learning is another term for

ILT (Information Learning Technologies), and ILT in its widest sense can be defined as:

> 'The use of technologies for effective teaching, learning and the management of learning.'

Here are a few more definitions:

> 'e-learning is the effective learning process created by combining digitally delivered content with (learning) support services.'
> West Yorkshire e-learning strategy

> 'DEL (distributed and electronic learning) can be represented as a spectrum ranging from supported distance learning in which the learner has limited physical contact with the tutor, to teacher-led, classroom-based activity which is interspersed with occasional or facilitated assignments.'
> DELG report

> 'Learning with the help of information and communication technology tools.'
> Get on with IT (Ferl, 2002)

> 'If someone is learning in a way that uses information and communication technologies, they are using e-learning. They could be a pre-school child playing an interactive game; they could be a group of pupils collaborating on a history project with pupils in another country via the Internet. They could be geography students watching an animated diagram of a volcanic eruption their tutor has just downloaded; they could be a nurse tasking her driving test online ... it all counts as e-learning.'
> Towards a Unified e-Learning Strategy (DfES, 2003)

Which definition do you work with?

What would your definition say? Would it be as wide-ranging as some of the definitions above, or would it be more specific? Does your model always have a tutor? This could be a physical or online presence. Does e-learning mean using the Internet, or just using a computer?

Most tutors take a broad view of e-learning, but tend to associate it with using a computer in a learning situation. There is no single correct answer, but discussing the meaning of e-learning with colleagues is a good way to start thinking about what you want it to achieve.

Why use e-learning?

e-learning is not an either/or way of learning. It is simply another tool or resource for tutors to use. The term 'blended' learning is a good description; a mixture of teaching and learning approaches that incorporates group work, textbooks and e-learning as and when appropriate. These are some of the benefits of e-learning outlined by outreach tutors:

> it increases the range and variety of approaches

> it enables learners who miss classes to catch up

> it means that learners can work at their own pace

> it gives fast/instant feedback to learners

> ICT skills become an additional 'accidental' skill for the learner

> it can make literacy, language and numeracy acceptable to some learners who would otherwise be embarrassed to attend courses

> it massively increases the resources and information sources available to learners and tutors

Blended learning

In most teaching situations, a tutor will use a variety of media and sources of information. These may include handouts, group discussions, video and the Internet. One medium blends into another; the thing they have in common is a topic or skill. Online resources will probably contribute to part, but not all, of your session. For much more information and guidance on blended learning, and e-learning in general, see e-guidelines 1, *Online Resources in the Classroom*, by Alan Clarke and Claudia Hesse (NIACE, 2004).

3
Why combine outreach and e-learning?

There are many reasons why learning providers are combining the strengths of outreach and e-learning. Outreach is an effective way of making contact with reluctant learners. e-learning has the potential to remove or reduce the barriers that many people face in taking part and succeeding in education.

For people to realise the full potential of technology in support of learning, a number of different things must be available. People need access to the Internet; the development of skills, both technical and learning, to confidently use technology; and help to understand the relevance of ICT to their lives.

It was the American report, *Falling Through the Net* (July 1999), which first coined the term 'the digital divide'. Although this is a US study, its findings and conclusions have been mirrored by subsequent UK reports and discussions.

> *'Failure to tackle the "digital divide" and increase ICT skills could reduce the nation's ability to compete effectively in an increasingly technological global economy. Employers are increasingly considering ICT skills when recruiting staff ... failure to tackle divides in the immediate future may entrench inequalities further with ICT being most effectively used by the most advantaged groups.'*
> (www.becta.org.uk/research/reports/docs/digitaldivide.pdf)

Research demonstrates that those people who have computer skills are becoming increasingly proficient, earning more money and accessing more and better services than those without such skills. The long-term consequences of ignoring the divide would be catastrophic for the individuals concerned and the economy.

4

Always start with the learner

If you are thinking about embarking on outreach and e-learning activities for the first time, or are looking to introduce e-learning into your current outreach provision, it is worth asking yourself *'What do I want to achieve by this?'* The answer to this question will help you to shape your learning offer. List all your answers to the questions. Take the first answer and ask 'how?' Don't stop with the first answer; keep on asking 'how' until you have an action plan. Then do the same with the next response, and so on.

The 'three hows': an example:

What do I want to achieve by this?

Answer:	Motivate learners.
How?	By providing interesting and exciting learning experiences.
How?	By making sure staff have the skills and resources to deliver an interesting and exciting learning experience.
How?	Involving staff in the E-Guides training programme or something similar. Making sure staff have time to identify good e-learning resources.

Often outreach and e-learning are developed in response to research that shows that one particular section of the community is not accessing learning. There are many reasons why this should be the case. Often people think of practical barriers to access, such as language barriers (learners speak little English), physical and practical barriers (such as mothers with small children, or disabled learners). There are, of course, many other barriers, some of which are very complex and deep rooted. People who have experienced failure in traditional learning environments as children will not, as adults, automatically turn to education for recreation and support. The act of taking learning into the community deinstitutionalises the learning experience; this is often accompanied by less formal styles of teaching and communication between tutors and learners. Peer mentors, volunteers and facilitators all contribute to make community learning a community experience.

> **Bishop Burton College** used UK online funds to buy mobile laptops to take around the rural East Riding of Yorkshire. They had recognised that women with young children found it difficult to attend college courses, so timed their mobile visit to match local playgroup sessions.

Who is your target group?

If you are working away from a main learning site, and want to work in the community to attract new learners, you may or may not have a particular group of learners in mind. Thinking through the following questions may help you develop provision.

> What is the make-up of the group?
> Where do they go?
> What will they be interested in?
> What services do they use, and who do they interact with?
> Who is already working with them?
> What would make life easier for them?
> Where do they shop?
> Where do they worship?
> Why would they want to learn in this group?
> How do I let them know I'm here?

How can ICT help them?

> Develop a website
> Design a community newsletter
> Shop online, online banking
> Hold a digital art event
> Find dress patterns
> Get an email address
> Find out about benefits, bus and train times, etc.
> Laptop loan scheme for flexible study
> Support adult basic skills

Researching your community

Wherever you are working, there will already be a huge amount of data available on the Internet about the local population. For further information visit the National Statistics site (**www.neighbourhood.statistics.gov.uk**). The Local Learning and Skills Council will hold a wealth of information about the local population, including work trends, social trends and skills gaps.

Involve learners in the design of your programme. Find out what they do and what they are interested in. Don't assume that you already know.

Every contact you have with your target group and local service providers is a development opportunity.

One of the ways of letting people know that you are there is to ask them what they want. A short flyer/questionnaire exploring what people would like to learn is a good start. Think about the way you will collect the information, e.g. provide a reply-paid envelope, a freepost address, or a post-box in local shops or centres. If people return your questionnaire, it's a bonus. The main thing is that they start to become aware that you are working in their area. The more you talk to people in the area, such as shopkeepers and service providers, the more people will see you as part of the local scene.

You may want to work with a particular group. In Settle, North Yorkshire, the local outreach team – supported by North Yorkshire County Council – started to work with local farmers in developing the use of ICT. Rather than a general-interest questionnaire, they devised a specific training needs analysis. This had many benefits. It was relevant and meaningful to the target group; it informed the content of the learning offer and built a bridge between the tutor and the learner before the programme started. This approach could work with any group.

The form goes on to ask about people's preferred style of learning, e.g. practical hands-on, one-to-one tuition, group work, or learning at

Training Requirements Form, Settle

Please tick the relevant box if you want to develop expertise in that area (or if you think others might)

☐ ☐ Farm paperwork, e.g. completing subsidy forms
☐ ☐ Simple farm accounts and records
☐ ☐ Selling directly to the customer using the Internet
☐ ☐ Writing successful planning applications
☐ ☐ Adding value to products
☐ ☐ Conservation work
Computer skills
Craftsman qualifications in
_____(specify)
Technical qualifications in
_____ (specify)
Opportunities in tourism
Identifying and maximising your assets
Understanding UK and EU farming legislation

Please tick where you would like your training to take place

☐ ☐ Settle High School
☐ ☐ Farm premises
☐ ☐ Auction mart
Village hall
Local pub
Other (please state)_____

home. It also asks about people's preferred day and time. Although it would probably not be possible to meet all the farmers' preferences, it's a good starting point for setting up a programme to meet most needs.

Photo Nick Hayes

5

The role of partners, networks and creative thinking!

It is clear when talking to successful project managers that good partnerships and networks are essential to successful community e-learning. Partners can provide a wide range of support, including technical skills and services, access to key target groups, venues in which to work, and funding routes.

Liverpool museums

Kate Johnson works for Liverpool Museums and could not operate without a pool of host organisations. Her outreach work is based around the use of Web technology to engage local community groups. Kate works in partnership with schools, local asylum seekers, ICT centres and community groups. The work is very creative and experimental. Although Kate is based in a museum she feels that outreach is valued by the organisation as a way of raising awareness of the museum service.

'Our job is not to sit on our laurels; our job is to bring people in … people will have a broader understanding of the museum through this project and know that it is there for them. You have to have the confidence to believe it will work and people are convinced when they see the results. You have to harness the skills already there; everyone exchanges skills; lifelong learning, family learning, volunteers, technical staff, and everyone can contribute.'

Coventry Adult Education Service (CAES)

CAES has around 100 learning centres in Coventry, of which approximately half have ICT equipment. The amount of equipment varies, depending on the size of the centre – some have fully equipped ICT suites; others have roaming laptops. Technical support is provided by the CAES as they have a technical support department to support schools. Some venues operate on a partnership basis and technical support is the partner's responsibility.

Sure Start approached CAES as they required a website for their project. Many Sure Starts across the country have paid professional website developers to create their websites, but here it was decided that the parents involved in Sure Start would embark on a learning programme themselves.

The group had various levels of ICT skills; some people did not want to get involved in the technical side of the development and therefore took on other roles, such as editing or the collation of information and/or content for the website.

The team went on to gain ICT and HTML skills, learn about Web design and digital photography, and in addition gained from pulling together as a team. The resulting website was a huge motivation factor for the group.

It is envisaged that some learners will progress to further training.

What does your network look like? Who is in it?

Many successful outreach e-learning projects are dependent on networks. Networks will include a wide range of organisations and each will bring skills, experience, expertise, sometimes money, and often access to more learners.

Look at the the puzzle on the facing page. If you have gaps in your network, try to think of a person or organisation that could work with you. At the same time, consider what you could offer them.

My Network

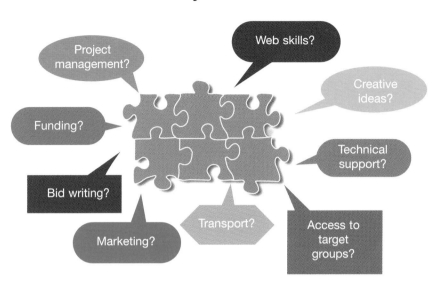

- Project management?
- Web skills?
- Creative ideas?
- Funding?
- Technical support?
- Bid writing?
- Marketing?
- Transport?
- Access to target groups?

Photo Nick Hayes

6

Staffing and support matters – the big picture

As well as expecting them to be excellent tutors, we often require outreach tutors who use ICT to perform a wide range of activities over and above teaching, such as carrying equipment or setting up a mobile wireless network. Take a few minutes to think about the possible experiences of a tutor running an average outreach e-learning session on behalf of your organisation.

The following list reflects findings from the research and indicates factors which need particular attention when using e-learning in outreach venues. Look at the checklist, go through each statement and select the appropriate check box, *yes*, *no*, or *don't know*. Although this exercise relates to tutors' experiences, it should also help to highlight aspects of your outreach e-learning provision that may need further development.

The questions are written for managers of outreach provision or those planning outreach. If you are a tutor, answer the questions from your own experience, e.g. *have you been given time to select/evaluate e-learning materials?*

Good Practice Check

Pre-session

yes no don't know

☐ ☐ ☐ The tutor has been given time to select/evaluate e-learning materials.

☐ ☐ ☐ e-learning resources are shared by tutors in your organisation.

☐ ☐ ☐ The organisation actively encourages the use of e-learning through target setting, and positive acknowledgement of tutors who use it.

☐ ☐ ☐ The tutor has had an ICT skills assessment and training needs analysis.

☐ ☐ ☐ The tutor can access training in e-learning and ICT skills.

☐ ☐ ☐ The tutor has had training in heavy lifting techniques.

☐ ☐ ☐ The tutor is aware of Health and Safety regulations with regard to using outreach venues.

☐ ☐ ☐ The tutor is able to anticipate and make reasonable adjustments to meet the needs of disabled learners.

☐ ☐ ☐ Tutors new to outreach are supported by their manager or a colleague at the outreach venue at their first learning session.

Getting there

yes   no   don't know

☐ ☐ ☐   The tutor has been given time to travel to the venue.

☐ ☐ ☐   The amount of equipment that your tutor transports is 'reasonable' (laptops, learning materials, CD-ROMS, cables and network connectors, wireless network, hearing loop, adaptive keyboards, tea/coffee, printers, scanners, paper).

☐ ☐ ☐   You are aware of the time it will take your tutor to collect, pack and unpack the equipment for his/her session.

Setting up

yes   no   don't know

☐ ☐ ☐   The venue will be open when the tutor arrives *or* the tutor has a key.

☐ ☐ ☐   There will be a technician to set up the equipment *or* the tutor is trained to set up the equipment.

☐ ☐ ☐   The tutor has the skills to load CD-ROMS onto laptops/computers or networks.

☐ ☐ ☐   When necessary, the tutor has admin. rights to use the computer network, can change screen settings, download plugins, etc.

☐ ☐ ☐   You know how long it takes your tutor to set up the equipment.

The venue

yes   no   don't know

yes	no	don't know	
☐	☐	☐	The venue complies with Health and Safety regulations.
☐	☐	☐	The tutor is aware of Health and Safety issues when using computers with groups.
☐	☐	☐	There is a procedure in place should a learner become ill.
☐	☐	☐	There is a procedure in place should the tutor become ill.
☐	☐	☐	The venue is warm and clean.
☐	☐	☐	The venue is appropriate for learners with disabilities.

Delivering the session

yes   no   don't know

yes	no	don't know	
☐	☐	☐	The tutor has been trained to provide technical support or can easily access it during sessions.
☐	☐	☐	The tutor's security in high-risk areas has been assessed.
☐	☐	☐	The tutor can support literacy, language and numeracy *or* there is a support process in place for outreach learners.
☐	☐	☐	There is appropriate support for less confident learners.
☐	☐	☐	There is access to information, advice and guidance.

Post-session

yes   no   don't know

yes	no	don't know	
☐	☐	☐	You know how long it takes your tutor to pack away the equipment.
☐	☐	☐	There is adequate provision for storage of equipment in a secure place.
☐	☐	☐	The equipment is insured.

Look back through your responses. Are there obvious areas where you could offer more support to outreach tutors or where your organisation could offer more support to you?

Are there better ways of organising outreach?

Research has shown that tutors find the off-site nature of outreach a hurdle causing frustration and difficulties. This is further exacerbated by the need for specialist skills, additional resources, or technical support associated with particular e-learning activities. The research highlighted issues around transport and making resources available to tutors, and good practice suggests that the following would be useful:

> Taxis to take equipment to and from venues on a regular schedule.

> Peripatetic technicians to transport and set up equipment before and after classes.

> The purchase of extra sets of equipment for busier centres, left on site in a laptop safe.

> Mobile phones for all outreach tutors.

> The sourcing and evaluation of e-learning resources as a regular team activity.

> The directing of tutors to specific resources that managers want them to use.

> The publication of all learning materials and documents on CD-ROMs or on a Learning Platform so that tutors can access them online.

Some of the alternative solutions may sound expensive, but a true cost/benefit evaluation of tutors' paid time and travel may show that there are more efficient and cost-effective ways of moving equipment from one venue to another.

7

The right person for the job

Many outreach managers recognised the difficulty of finding staff with such a wide range of skills, and decided to grow their own!

Outreach and e-learning tutors are expected to perform a wide range of tasks, often working part time and in isolation. Many outreach providers have developed local 'Learning Champions' to assist tutors. These champions are sometimes paid for their time, or may be volunteers.

Leeds College of Technology

Brenda Barnett ran a project funded by the Learning & Skills Council (LSC) (co-financing). The project was called 'Bridging the Gap' and was aimed at training people to become Adult Learning Support Assistants in community-based IT learning centres. The target group included employed (low-skilled, low-paid) and unemployed people.

Its aim was to provide them with ICT qualifications at whatever level they needed, e.g. CLAIT, CLAIT+, ECDL. They then went on a six-week course to gain NVQ Level 3 in Direct Training and Support. Some participants have gone on to do a Level 4 qualification. The idea was that the participants would be fully trained to work in centres and act as role models to the local learners.

Some of the recruits on the programme started as learners in ICT centres, went on to get ICT qualifications, plus the NVQ Level 3 training and support qualification, and then were able to teach at the centres from which they were originally recruited. One trainee was a chef who was unhappy at work; he joined the scheme, gained the NVQ support qualification, and is now teaching cookery in a special (needs) school. Another was a bus driver who is now looking after the learning centre within his company.

In Settle, North Yorkshire, the outreach team manager recognised that local champions had a key role to play in encouraging the uptake of e-learning by local communities, and that if they were to continue to be effective, a good champion support programme would have to be put in place. Champions are paid, but may work anything from 5 to 15 hours a week. They come from the local community and their role is to informally raise awareness and encourage people to take up learning. This may be by writing articles for the local press, visiting community groups, attending local events and generally having a high profile and talking about learning in the Settle area.

Skills development

The E-Guides programme, devised and delivered by NIACE, supports the development of e-learning skills in people working in the ACL sector. The programme aims to increase the use of e-learning by developing the skills and knowledge of E-Guides to support colleagues from all subject areas. The course comprises an initial three-day training programme and participants will go on to cascade the skills they have learned throughout their own organisation. Further information is available at AClearn (**www.aclearn.net**).

The Learning & Skills Development Agency (LSDA) are running a parallel pilot scheme aimed at engaging Skills for Life tutors in e-learning. This is a peer-support, modular programme delivered over a period of time, ensuring that tutors acquire and implement a range of skills for engaging in e-learning. Modules include 'Creative use of the Internet', 'Delivering On-screen National Tests', 'Using ICT Communications in Teaching and Learning', and 'Digital Imaging and Simple ICT Tools in Teaching and Learning', among others.

The Ferl Practitioners' Programme has been created by the British Educational Communications and Technology Agency (Becta) to equip the teaching, learning resources, learning support and technical staff in the further education and Lifelong Learning sectors with the skills necessary to harness the potential of ILT and e-learning. Further information is available on the Ferl (formerly Further Education Resources for Learning) site (**www.ferl.becta.org.uk**).

There are a number of organisations that have developed competencies for new technologies:

> The FENTO ILT standards for the application of ICT to teaching and supporting learning and management in further education are downloadable from the ILT section of the FENTO (Further Education National Training Organisation) site (**www.fento.ac.uk**).

> The Institute of IT Training Competencies that include competencies for trainers, developers, designers, e-tutors and e-learning materials (**www.iitt.org.uk/public/about/aims.asp**).

> The IT Sector Skills Council has developed the E-skills Passport described as an IT User Skills Framework, developed in response to consultation with over 900 employers and stakeholders. The Framework identifies the skills required by non-professionals to use computer hardware and software and electronic communications effectively at home, school or work. The Framework is broken down into five categories: User, Inexperienced, Foundation, Intermediate, Advanced and Expert. It also identifies different types of IT 'techniques': operating a computer, troubleshooting, maintenance, security, Internet and the Web, email, word-processing, spreadsheets, databases, Web design, and art and design. To find out more go to **www.e-skills.com/e-skillspassport**

Changing the way you work

If you are a manager, it is important to involve everyone in the change as early as possible. Imposed change is hard on everyone. From the NIACE research, the best way to ensure effective take up of e-learning seems to be a consultative approach, with opportunities for all staff to contribute. Show that you listen to ideas, and give feedback on ideas that are not taken up. *Compliance* may be enough, but *commitment* is better.

If you are a tutor, find out about any changes happening in your workplace. Many of the e-learning Champions who participated in the NIACE research had created the role because of their own interest in ICT, not as the result of a job description or organisational requirements.

One of the clear messages from the research was that respondents felt there should be a skills transfer from technical staff to tutors and that *all* tutors should have basic technical skills to survive. The view was also expressed that incorporating ICT into courses gave the courses more credibility.

The extent of e-learning in a programme is usually governed more by the tutor's awareness of what is available than any other factor. Very few organisations are involved in creating their own e-learning materials. However, the E-Guides pilot review showed that one of the most popular aspects of training was learning how to quickly create simple interactive worksheets in Word! For more on creating content see e-guidelines 3, *Developing your own e-learning materials*, by Shubhanna Hussain (published by NIACE, 2004).

The following key points about staff training were highlighted in the NIACE research:

> All tutors need basic technical skills, such as being able to install an external CD-ROM drive.
> Nervous tutors make dependent learners – if e-learning is to be successful, it is vital for tutors to have the confidence to use ICT equipment.
> Tutors will only use e-learning resources if they have had the time to find them, evaluate them and feel confident about them.
> PowerPoint may be a good stepping-stone to the creation of interactive learning resources for tutors who are reluctant to pick up general ICT skills.

> There are lots of good free e-resources available, but many tutors are unaware of them.

> Start staff training slowly; build confidence.

Although many of these points seem obvious, acting on the issues they raise is often not straightforward. *A slow and systematic staff training and support programme* in conjunction with *time for staff to source and evaluate e-learning resources* would seem to be the essential elements of a successful outreach and e-learning programme.

8

Tracking learners and their progress

One area that technology can support is tracking, learning and keeping management information up to date. Various funding bodies require the numbers of learners to be logged, and a variety of methods are used, often involving lots of paper.

Some ACL providers use Web-based learning platforms to monitor learners' progress and store resources, such as a Virtual Learning Environment (VLE). A VLE is a software package that manages, supports, tracks and records learner progress electronically. There are a number of VLE software packages available, including Blackboard, WebCT and Lotus LearningSpace. To find out more about learning platforms visit AClearn (**www.aclearn.net**).

A recent e-focus group looking at outreach and the use of VLEs agreed that VLEs should be designed to be accessed by a dial-up telephone link! The issues they faced were not those of technology and high bandwidth but of training staff to create work in small files, and to use the VLE for communications. Staff should recognise that learners may access the VLE from home, the library, the local café, or a mobile phone connection. It has to be 'fit for purpose'!

Buckinghamshire Adult Learning have introduced smartcards across the whole service for their adult learning provision which takes place in over 150 centres, many of which are outreach facilities.

The system allows learners to select which type of learner they are, e.g. UK online, learndirect, etc., and, depending on the data needs for that programme, they are asked appropriate registration questions. Once the answers to these questions have been entered, a learner agreement is signed by the learner, a smartcard produced and a password allocated. The learner keeps and uses the smartcard to log on to the system each time they attend a training session, using a smartcard reader attached to every computer.

It has extensive facilities, only some of which have yet been piloted. Questionnaires can be added to the system to collect information from learners, e.g. satisfaction surveys; users can be prompted to enter details when they next use the system or after logging on to the system a fixed number of times. The system can broadcast messages, log packages that have been used by learners, and has the potential to manage individual learning plans for each learner.

Learners have been very positive about the system. Generally people find paper forms onerous to complete, but this engages learners immediately, and produces an instant card for them to take away, giving them immediate ownership of their learning.

Photo Nick Hayes

9
Finding e-learning materials

One of the biggest barriers that tutors face when introducing e-learning is finding the right resources to use. Trying out, evaluating and incorporating e-learning is initially time-consuming but pays off in the medium and long term.

Free resources

The Internet is awash with resources. However, selecting good, appropriate resources takes time. Here are some of the sites you might want to look at for free learning materials.

> The *Learning Content* section of AClearn (**www.aclearn.net**) provides access to National Learning Network (NLN) materials and the Resource Exchange. The NLN has developed over 500 hours of e-learning materials across a wide range of subjects and is commissioning more in 2004. The materials are categorised into ten curriculum areas. Materials have been created in small 'episodes', each taking about 20–30 minutes to complete. The resource exchange provides access to content and resources hosted on the website or linked from elsewhere, allowing selection by subject area. The site also allows practitioners to host their own content to share with other practitioners.

> The Ferl site (**ferl.becta.org.uk**) hosts 'Store Cupboard', a bank of teaching resources that can be used over and over again by practitioners. The resources are copyright free and downloadable. Files are sorted into type, such as audio and video, images, quizzes, etc.

> Many tutors love the BBC learning website
(**www.bbc.co.uk/learning/courses**). The BBC boasts interactive
learning materials in a number of categories, including gardening,
health, history and languages, and the materials range from
complete courses to small interactive units. Self-assessment is
available in the languages section to enable learners to select the
right level of course. The courses are often linked to popular TV
programmes and include familiar presenters. Most tutors who use e-
learning have at some point used the BBC's Becoming Web Wise CD-
ROM. This has proved to be an excellent starting point for tutors
and learners who want to find out more about the Internet.

For much more on free resources see e-guidelines 1, *Online Resources
in the Classroom*, by Alan Clarke and Claudia Hesse (NIACE, 2004).

Getting started

In the next section you will find a selection of free e-learning
materials to evaluate and use. Try to set aside some time for you and
your colleagues to look at these resources.

> Use the evaluation table to get you started (p. 31). Look at a range
of resources and score them against the criteria for suitability for
your learners.
> Get into the habit of sharing e-learning resources with colleagues.
Set aside a regular time to review. This may be face to face or by
email, whichever is the most appropriate.
> Agree with your colleagues to try out different e-learning resources,
and systematically get feedback and log your experiences and your
learners' responses to your resources. Keep a list of the resources
used, together with the responses. This will be invaluable for new
tutors or tutors new to e-learning.

Evaluating e-learning

Set aside an hour. Select three resources from the list below. Open up each resource and work through it for 15 minutes. Assess the module against the criteria in the training evaluation form on the facing page. Think about the quality of the resource; how and when you would use it. What does it offer over and above your current resources?

www.bbc.co.uk/webwise
www.thestudyplace.org/welcome.taf
www.mathslessons.co.uk
www.bbc.co.uk/skillswise
www.spelling.hemscott.net/exlist.html
www.learnthenet.com/english/animate.htm
www.funbrain.com/teachers/index.html
www.qax.org/driving/quiz1.html
www.askoxford.com
www.drugworld.org
web.uvic.ca/hrd/halfbaked
www.lwts.org.uk/Action4learning/write/W002.html
www.plainenglish.co.uk/guides.html
www.thepaperboy.com
www.moneymatterstome.co.uk
a4esl.org
showcase.commedia.org.uk

Searching for resources on the Internet

> Start with a good search engine such as Google (www.Google.com). This is very popular, but others (such as www.AskJeeves.co.uk) are also easy to use.
> Use nouns and keywords in your query. This will reduce the number of items found, but of those, some should be relevant!
> Use the asterisk * after your search term (e.g. microphone*) to tell the search engine to match all words that start with these letters. It will pick up plural and singular versions.
> Combine keywords into phrases to narrow your search by using quotation marks, e.g. "Norman architecture".
> Use the plus and minus signs. A plus sign before a word means the search must include that word, and a minus sign indicates a word to exclude, e.g. "paradise island"–Bahamas+Maldives should return websites for paradise island in the Maldives rather than the Bahamas.

Evaluating e-learning resources: sample evaluation form

Name:

Resource:

URL:

Date evaluated:

		Comments A	Comments B	Comments C
Target audience	Who is it aimed at?			
Subject	Topic covered			
Usage	When would you use it?			
		A score 1–5	*B score 1–5*	*C score 1–5*
Content	Is it relevant to the topic and to your learners?			
	Does it enhance the curriculum?			
Learning approach	Is it clear? Does it build skills or information, rather than being haphazard and confusing? Does it point to additional learning or information sources?			
Appearance/ Design	Is it pleasing to look at, not too bright, garish, messy, or cluttered? Has it a consistent style?			
Navigation	Is it easy and clear to use? Do all action buttons work, and are they easy to see? Is it easy to move around the site, exit and move on?			

95641

If you try this exercise, you will have evaluated some e-learning 'content'. Now select the content you think you or a colleague could use. Think of a specific scenario, a lesson where you might include it. Consider how you will make it available:

> How will you introduce it, and what follow-up work will you do on completion?
> Will it enhance and extend your lesson?
> Will it enable learners who do not attend to catch up?
> Will it add a 'fun' element to your course?
> What skills do learners need in order to use it?

While it seems clear that e-learning has a lot to offer learners, it is less clear what is expected of tutors. For many tutors, e-learning means that the tutor becomes a learner and has to pick up a wide range of new skills very quickly. Fortunately, the overwhelming message from outreach tutors who use e-learning is: *'you don't have to do everything at once'!* Start slowly, in a way that you feel comfortable with. Remember, e-learning is not about ICT, it's about supporting learning. Familiarise yourself with a few good e-learning resources.

Things to consider

> Set up a system for gathering information about resources on the Internet.
> With your colleagues, devise an effective way of evaluating and logging resources.
> With your colleagues, devise an effective way of evaluating the use of e-learning, e.g. learner evaluation, impact on learning
> Monitor how learners respond to specific e-learning resources.

10
Creating your own resources

Creating interactive worksheets is not as difficult as people think. Word, Excel and PowerPoint all enable you to create interesting interactive worksheets.

Word Worksheets	**www.Learningtechnologies.ac.uk** have excellent instructions for tutors who want to create their own interactive worksheets. The materials are free to ACL providers. Follow the link and download 'Using Microsoft Office to Create Interactive Learning Materials – Microsoft Word'.
Ferl	You will find lots of instructions and examples of homegrown interactive worksheets on the Ferl website (**www.ferl.becta.org.uk**). Select 'Teaching and Learning' and then 'Resource Creation'. You can choose to learn how to create interactive worksheets, presentations and spreadsheets by following video or text instructions. You can also view lots of examples of worksheets created by tutors on the Ferl site.
PowerPoint	This is an excellent tool for tutors and learners. Have a look at another example from the Ferl website: 'Journey along the river Ystwyth'.
Quizzes	These are quick and easy to put together with Hot Potato (**web.uvic.ca/hrd/halfbaked**). Follow this link and download the software to your desktop. The instructions are clear and easy to follow.
Webquests	In the mid 1990s an American teacher created the concept of a learning activity whereby most or all of the information used by the learner was

obtained from the Internet. The name of this
activity was a Webquest. Creating a Webquest is a
structured activity. You can find a toolkit for
building Webquests on AClearn
(**aclresources.net/webquests**). To see a range of
webquests go to Webquest (**webquest.org**).

If you or your colleagues would like to pick up the skills to develop
e-learning content, numerous courses are available. You will find a
few of these listed below, but there are many more. Try spreading the
new skills across your team so that you can teach each other.

Here are just a few examples of courses for tutors who want to create
their own content.

Course	Provider	URL
Designing E- learning	learndirect	**www.learndirect.co.uk/learn/courses**
Designing and Writing E- learning content	Sherpa Integrated Learning Ltd	**www.sherpa.org.uk**
TONIC	The Online Netskills Interactive Course	**www.netskills.ac.uk/TonicNG**
The Online Tutor – Screencraft and Preparing Content	learndirect	**www.learndirect.co.uk/learn/courses**
Learning to Teach On-line (LeTTOL)	Sheffield College	**www.sheffcol.ac.uk/lettol/facts/ structure.html**
Certificate in Transforming Learning with ILT	Ferl	**www.jeb.co.uk/TLILT2003.asp**

In 2003 the National Learning Network made a small sum of money
available to local authorities to purchase authoring tools for ACL
practitioners. A summary of these tools used can be found at AClearn
(**www.aclearn.net/content/tacl/about**).

For more on creating content and on the use of digital cameras see e-
guidelines 2, *Digital cameras in teaching and learning*, by Phil
Hardcastle, and e-guidelines 3, *Developing your own e-learning
materials*, by Shubhanna Hussain (both published by NIACE, 2004).

11

e-learning, outreach and Skills for Life

Government statistics show that one in five people cannot read or write as well as an average 11-year-old. This means that at least one in five people walking through the doors of community-based outreach provision may have a literacy or numeracy need. Some learners, however, will not openly access literacy or numeracy classes for fear of stigmatisation, but will be attracted to ICT training. With the recognition that technology can be used as a motivational and teaching tool, Skills for Life training can be provided through ICT, which can have a real impact on the learning experiences and achievements of Skills for Life learners.

Some of the advantages of using e-learning in outreach highlighted by our research were:

> increases participation, attracts more learners,

> increases confidence,

> enhances teaching methods; is interactive and user friendly

> increases motivation,

> gives access to a wide range of learning materials for other subjects, e.g. ESOL,

> is able to offer a wide range of courses that are needs-led.

Try it yourself:

Get learners to collect samples of text in electronic form, e.g. Internet news reports, hobby pages, general interest information, etc. Cut and paste these into MS Word. Click on Tools, then on AutoSummarize, then select the type of summary you want. This will provide a computer-generated précis of the document. A discussion can take place around the principles of précis work, skim reading and scanning, giving plenty of scope for discussion.

E-learning can be used to motivate and engage Skills for Life learners, and provide access to a range of online resources for use online or offline, downloadable resources, or simply the use of various forms of technology in effective and creative ways.

This has been achieved by a national pilot scheme such as the E-Learning for Skills for Life Tutors Programme managed by the LSDA. This is aimed at training practitioners in using e-learning to manage, deliver and support Skills for Life provision. Availability of technology and access to the Internet in outreach venues has meant that Skills for Life learners can engage in e-learning, and can include activities such as:

> Using online national tests – a sample test is available at (**www.dfes.gov.uk/readwriteplus**).

> Using digital images and video to personalise materials and introduce an element of interest and fun into teaching. Windows XP has a simple to use video editor called Windows Movie Maker, usually found in Programs, Accessories in the Windows Start menu.

> Effective use of the Internet to seek appropriate and suitable resources for the target group. Use double quotation marks and plus and minus signs to refine your searches, e.g. "basic skills"+resources–children in the search engine will generate a few hundred thousand hits when searching for adult basic skills resources, whereas the words 'basic skills' on their own will generate millions of hits.

> Use of special features in commonly available software, such as MS Office, to create interesting interactive resources.

> Using the Internet as a resource for accessibility awareness training using online videos, demonstrations and simulations (see chapter 13, p. 43 for more details).

Photo Nick Hayes

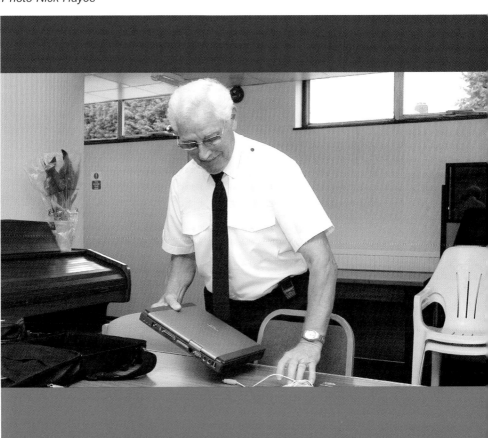

12

Selecting and using equipment

A key ingredient for e-learning is having access to the right technical equipment. A great deal can be done with basic standard equipment, i.e. computers or laptops, generally available software, and a printer. However, a lot more can be achieved by adding additional items. A balance has to be struck between what you need to enhance the learner experience and how much you have to spend.

If you are buying computers or portable systems for the first time, take advice. Find a friendly expert in your own or a partner's organisation. If that's not possible, consider paying for independent

Carrying laptops

Anne Chester is the ICT Organiser working for the Redcar Adult Learning Service. The service she provides operates in 70 venues throughout Redcar, which include rural centres, pubs, community rooms, church halls, sheltered housing, libraries and five learning centres. Transporting laptops was a major problem. Anne searched various sites and found the perfect solution – a trolley that tutors could use to move laptops from their car to the venue and back. The one she selected is foldable and lightweight. Anne also recognised that moving equipment around puts a physical strain on tutors. All her outreach tutors take part in a 'heavy lifting' training programme. This is a one-day course provided by her local Borough Council.

advice, or make use of free advice from websites such as
www.aclearn.net or **www.helpisathand.gov.uk** You may wish to
try your local authority, or Business Link, to find the names of people
who can offer objective impartial advice. *Insist that they are not linked
to a supplier.*

An impartial adviser will have no reason to encourage you to spend
more money than you need to. You and they will want to consider:

> Computer/laptop specification, that is, the size of its memory, type
  of processor, etc., based on what you want it to do.
> Peripherals such as digital cameras, scanners and printers.
> Wireless keyboards and mice for learners who may find the
  keyboard and mice alternatives on a laptop difficult to use.
> CD writers and flash memory for file transfers.
> A data projector or interactive whiteboard.
> Networking options – wireless, mobile phone, broadband,
  telephone dial-up.
> Connection to the Internet, and firewalls.
> Storage, transport and security.
> Software licences for both operating systems, e.g. Windows, and
  applications software such as Microsoft Word or Microsoft Office.
> Enabling technologies for disabled learners – screen readers, voice-
  recognition software, laptop overlays. You can find information on a
  wide range of adaptive technologies from Ability Net
  (**www.abilitynet.com**) Look at their free skills and fact sheets.
> The weight of laptops. You can buy very lightweight laptops but
  often the CD-ROM drive and batteries are separate. This means in
  practice that there are more components to lose and the overall
  weight may not be much lighter than a standard laptop.
> Maintenance contracts, warranties and support from the supplier.

Here is a shopping list from an experienced ACL provider who purchased the equipment in March 2004. It includes most of the basic hardware you would need to set up a portable laptop wireless network with ten people in mind.

> 10 Pentium 3 laptop computers with modem + MS Office Software /Windows XP
> wireless network cards
> hub
> access port
> portable scanner
> 4 Epson C62 printers (or equivalent)
> 10 carry cases
> digital projector + portable screen

The *technical guidance* section on the AClearn website (**www.aclearn.net**) has information on the types of peripherals you may want to consider to engage tutors and learners in e-learning. Here are some of these:

Scanners: as well as scanning pictures from any printed material, e.g. magazines, it is much more interesting to scan everyday items which have a reasonably flat surface that will fit on the platen of a scanner, e.g. leaves, feathers, money, mobile phone text messages – the options are endless and perfect for creating worksheets.

Digital cameras: compared to conventional cameras these are instant, and involve no film processing. Once the images have been downloaded onto the computer, you can make as many copies as you like, make images larger or smaller, and manipulate them in a graphics package. Images can then be transferred to other packages such as Microsoft Word or PowerPoint. Learners can create electronic photo albums, email photos to relatives, and create digital art. See Hussain (2004) for much more on digital cameras.

Digital video cameras: these are ideal for capturing movement and recording processes. They give numerous possibilities for the tutor and learners, such as recording movement of the mouth for pronunciation, body language, aspects of festivals and celebrations or cultural behaviour, making things, dance movements – again, the options are endless. Editing videos is not as difficult as you might think. Computers with Windows XP usually come with free Windows Movie Maker; ask your technical staff to show you how to download video clips from your digital video camera and show you how to use Windows Movie Maker to enable you to incorporate video into your learning materials or lesson plans.

Display Screen Technology: these include data projectors, touch screens, interactive whiteboards and similar devices such as Mimio or CleverBOARD. They allow for smart delivery of training but, more importantly, can allow learners to interact with the display in a group setting, e.g. when using an interactive whiteboard.

Mobile phones: text messaging is something the younger generation have mastered – they have even developed their own 'language' of abbreviated words. Text messaging for adult learners can provide another means of communication, and can encourage communication between the generations. Text messaging can be particularly useful for learners who have hearing impairments.

A recent survey of ACL tutors revealed that most thought outreach tutors should have some technical skills. In particular they thought that tutors should be able to set up a wireless network, download plugins, use external peripherals and drives and access the Internet.

It is difficult to talk about computers without using jargon. Jargon is more than a new language; in some cases the new words represent a whole new concept. Don't panic! There are a few words that will come up time and time again, and we give a glossary of some of these at the end of this guide. When discussing computers with an adviser, ask them to explain any terms you don't understand. It's not unusual to find that they also struggle to explain exactly what a word means!

If you want to use e-learning resources, it is essential to select your equipment to meet at least the minimum standards required to make effective use of the resources available. Descriptions and specifications of equipment can be found in the NIACE publication *A Guide to Outreach with Laptops* (Word, 200).

A recurring concern in outreach is technical support. Some organisations employ their own technician to set up and dismantle mobile networks in outreach venues, but they seem to be in the minority. Others have a peripatetic technician who covers a number of centres. Some work with partner organisations and pay nominal amounts for technical support, or include their costs within a project bid.

In Bradford a local project decided to meet the need in an innovative and cost-effective way.

Computing Bradford (ComB)

This was a small project set up in 1996 with ERDF funds and matched funding in kind, employing one person to provide technical telephone support. The project has gone from strength to strength, and now employs four people full time and provides on-the-job training for trainees.

The project supports 1,200 computers in 200 community voluntary-sector organisations across West Yorkshire, providing on-site and telephone support, plus other technical services such as building and supplying PCs, enabling organisations to get Internet accounts, and so on. The service varies, depending on need, and can range from a simple installation of anti-virus software or a computer health check, to wiring and equipping complete training suites.

Half of the running costs of the organisation come from subscriptions, an hourly charge and the supply of services. The other half comes from project funding from sources such as ERDF, NRF, local authority community funds, and so on. The projects add a new dimension to the work – for example, they have provided on-the-job experience to 22 trainees from New Deal, IteC and various colleges. An ERDF project has provided training places for 16–18-year-olds who have an interest in ICT but no experience; they have attended courses at the college (one day) and received four days' on-the-job training per week at ComB. The trainees receive a wage, a pension and a reference when they leave. Many have gone on to full-time jobs.

The aim of the service is not to make huge amounts of profit but work towards sustainability, and the ethos of the project is to enable community and voluntary-sector organisations to use ICT effectively.

13

Accessibility

People often assume that supporting learners with additional requirements is costly and should be left to specialists. There is no doubt that specialist organisations are better equipped, e.g. have good resources, and appropriately skilled staff to support disabled people or people with additional needs. However, all practitioners can go a long way to being inclusive.

Tutors working in outreach centres are less likely to have institutional support available for additional needs than centres based in mainstream venues, where there are other support services available. There is, therefore, a greater need for tutors working in outreach venues to have disability awareness training.

Some simple guidelines:

> Be polite and treat people with respect.
> Treat people as you would want to be treated.
> Treat people as individuals; treat adults as adults.
> Relax and just be you.
> Don't make assumptions.
> Ask what support the learner needs.
> Listen and understand.
> Know your own limitations, and seek advice if necessary.

Much of the software available nowadays comes with inbuilt accessibility options, i.e. allowing resizing of fonts, changing foreground and background colours to allow for different contrasts,

Accessibility solutions at no cost

There are facilities inherent in common software which can be used at no cost to support learners. Find out more from the section 'My Computer My Way' on Ability Net (**www.abilitynet.co.uk**) and accessibility information provided by Microsoft on
www.microsoft.com/enable/training/default.aspx

Accessibility demonstrations using simulations:

www.webaim.org/simulations/lowvision

www.webaim.org/simulations/screenreader

www.webaim.org/simulations/cognitive

www.drc.org.uk/newsroom/interactive.asp

Disability Discrimination Act (1995)

The Disability Rights Commission has produced a post-16 code of practice (code COPP 16), which is a useful interpretation and guidance for practitioners. It is available from The Disability Rights Commission (**www.drc-gb.org**).

etc. There are also range of accessibility options which require the purchase of equipment, i.e. hardware and software. Often assistive technology is associated with high-tech solutions which can sometimes be expensive and require specialist knowledge to implement and operate, and are usually specific to particular impairments. In such cases it is recommended that you seek help from specialists who provide advice on such matters. However, low-tech equipment can also have significant impact for learners with minor impairments/disabilities, and is often easy to obtain and usually at a low cost, e.g. wrist rests, lap trays, non-slip mats, tracker balls, etc. The Techdis accessibility database (**www.techdis.ac.uk**) has a comprehensive list of assistive equipment. More information can be found in the *Technology and Disability* section of AClearn (**www.aclearn.net**).

14

Connectivity

The presence or absence of an Internet connection dramatically impacts on the resources available to your learners. A single telephone line will enable you to connect one computer to the Internet. This could be useful as a central resource and to demonstrate via a projector, but downloading files will be very slow and can be off-putting for learners. For many learners it will resemble the type of connection they have or could have at home. However, learners are increasingly moving to home broadband and may actually have a faster link at home than in your centre!

Some things to consider

> Choosing an Internet Service Provider (ISP)

> Mobile Internet connectivity

> Broadband

> Remote access

> Wireless Local Area Networks (WLANs)

> Satellite communications

> Wireless Wide Area Networks (WWANs)

> Managed services

> Security and Internet safety

> Caching

Guide to connectivity based on learndirect minimum requirements

Number of computers	Internet connection
1	Dial-up over normal phone line
2	Dial-up OK sharing normal phone line although performance could be slow
3–6	ISDN2 line, 2 lines at 64kbps provides 128kbps in total
7–9	ISDN6 line, 374 kbps
9–14	256 kbps Lease Line per annum unlimited access
15–20	512 kbps Lease Line per annum unlimited access
20–40	1 mbps Lease Line
40–60	2 mbps Lease Line
60–80	2 mbps Lease Line

If you would like to know more about the different ways of connecting your computers to the Internet, go to the Technical Information section at Becta (**getconnected.ngfl.gov.uk**), or the *Information and Resources* section of Help is at Hand (**www.helpisathand.gov.uk**).

If you are developing an Internet Acceptable Use Policy, Becta have developed an excellent game called Superhighway Safety; find it on Help is at Hand (**www.helpisathand.gov.uk/info/print/publications/safety**).

Connectivity in a rural area: The WON 'I Can Do IT Project' Adult and Community Learning – South Dartmoor Community College, Ashburton, Devon

The rationale for using a satellite broadband Internet access system was based on the difficulties communicating across the southern half of Dartmoor. The catchment area for South Dartmoor Community College and the Adult and Community Learning Department extends from the A38 up to the high moor. There is a marked reluctance for parents, carers and others to travel more than 20 minutes during the school day and at night. Broadband at the time was difficult to obtain, and is still not readily accessible to the isolated as well as larger communities.

Generally across Dartmoor mobile phone connectivity is poor and there are a number of test cases still pending as regards the siting of masts – especially of the Tetra variety.

Using a satellite-based system to give the community the chance to use broadband to assist in their application for dedicated exchanges and to upgrade general skills seemed logical, therefore. The system is unusual in that the normal configuration is a coach or bus that is adapted to hold, as a rule, six computers. It has a tutor or similar member of staff and 'calls' at venues on a regular basis, or by request.

Its availability and venues being governed by vehicle access, the project opted for a small vehicle – in this case a Renault Kangoo – with a satellite dish on the roof, capable of carrying all the computers and printer, etc., for delivering courses at any location, regardless of the remoteness. The vehicle also carries a petrol-driven generator to supply power where mains power is unavailable.

15 Glossary of terms

For the full glossary or to find out more about any of the terms listed, go to AClearn (www.aclearn.net/technical/glossary)

Assistive technology	Specialised equipment and software used to maintain or improve the functional capabilities of a person with a disability.
Browser	A program that enables you to read Web pages (i.e. it decodes HTML). The most common are Microsoft Internet Explorer and Netscape Navigator.
CD-R	A compact disc that can have information written to it by a CD writer. Some, but not all computers have CD writers built in. You can only write to it once.
CD-RW	Similar to a CD-R but can be reused over and over again.
Connectivity	Describes the method you use to connect your computer to the Internet
Digital camera	Saves pictures to a smartcard rather than film. The images from the smartcard can be transferred to a computer for editing and enhancement.
Domain Name System (DNS)	Operates as an address on the Internet.
Hardware	The computer equipment itself: monitor, keyboard, printer, etc.
HTML	Hypertext Mark-up Language. A code used to create Web documents and enable browsers to read them.
Hub	A hardware device that joins several strands of a network together. A junction.
ISP	Internet Service Provider. A company providing connections to the Internet, such as Freeserve.

LAN	Local Area Network. A series of computers linked together locally, e.g. in a classroom. Computers can share files and printers, etc.
Modem	Used to transmit digital information across an analogue channel such as a phone line.
Multi media	Systems that use a wide range of media, e.g. video, audio, text, graphics.
Networking	The way one computer links to another and to shared hardware such as a printer. A common mistake is to think that you need a printer for every computer: several computers can be linked through a network to one printer or to the Internet.
Notebook	A portable computer or laptop.
Operating system	Controls the higher functions of a computer. Microsoft Windows is the most common.
PDA	Personal Digital Assistant. Hand-held computer. Often designed to synchronise diary and contact functions with a PC via a device called a cradle.
Peripherals	Equipment that you add on to your computer, e.g. digital camera, scanner, etc.
Plasma Screen	Large, flat, thin TV screen. Can be used as a monitor.
Plugins	Software that you *download* from the Internet to enable your computer to run some programs, e.g. Acrobat Reader.
Router	Hardware or software that determines where data coming from one network is sent.
Software	Makes the computer work. Covers the basic *operating* software and *applications*, such as Microsoft Word or Microsoft Office.
URL	Uniform Resource Locator. The Internet address usually seen at the top of a Web page, usually preceded by 'www'.
WAN	Wide Area Network. Series of computers linked together over a wide area, e.g. the Internet.

Abbreviations

NLN	National Learning Network
NRF	Neighbourhood Renewal Fund
VLE	Virtual Learning Environment

16 Bibliography

Clarke, A. (1999) *How to Create Effective Information and Communication Technology Learning Programmes – A Guide*, Leicester: NIACE.

Clarke, A. (2001) *First Steps – Initial Information and Communications Technologies (ICT) Events*, Leicester: NIACE.

Clarke, A. (2002) *Online Learning Skills*, Leicester: NIACE.

Clarke, A. (2002) *Online Learning and Social Exclusion*, Leicester: NIACE.

Clarke, A. and Englebright, L. (2003) *ICT: The New Basic Skill*, Leicester: NIACE.

Clarke, A., Essom, J. and Forty, V. (1999) *Developing Skills for Information Technology Tutors*, Leicester: NIACE.

Clarke, A. and Hesse, C. (2004) *Online Resources in the Classroom: A practical guide on using the Word Wide Web to deliver and support adult learning*, Leicester: NIACE.

DfES (2003) T*owards a Unified Learning Strategy*, avaialable at www.dfes.gov.uk/consultations2/16 (accessed 20 October 2004).

Ferl (2002) *Get On With It*. available at www.ferl.becta.org.uk/display.cfm?resid=3939 (accessed 20 October 2004).

Hardcastle, P. (2004) *Digital cameras in teaching and learning*, Leicester: NIACE.

Hussain, S. (2004) *Developing your own e-learning materials*: *Applying user-centred design techniques to creating learning materials for adults*, Leicester: NIACE.

ILEA: Taubman, D., Nicholls, S., Murray, E., Clarke, K., Cushman, M., Anders, J. (2000) *Aylesbury Revisited : Outreach in the 1980s*, Leicester: NIACE.

McGivney, V. (2000) *Recovering Outreach : Concepts, Issues and Practices*, Leicester: NIACE.

McGivney, V. (2000) *Working with Excluded Groups: guidelines on good practice for providers and policy-makers in working with groups under-represented in adult learning : based on the Oxfordshire Widening Partcipation Project*, Leicester: NIACE.

McGivney, V. (2002) *Spreading the Word : Reaching Out to New Learners*, Leicester: NIACE.

National Research and Development Centre for Adult Literacy and Numeracy, Institute of Education and Basic Skills Agency (2003) *Using Laptop Computers to Develop Basic Skills : A Handbook for Practitioners*, London: NRDC Publications, available at: www.nrdc.org.uk/uploads/documents/doc_2838.pdf (accessed 17 September 2004).

Newman, M. (1979) *The Poor Cousin : a study of adult education*, London: Allen and Unwin.

Watson, A. and Tyers, C. (1998) *Demonstration Outreach Projects: Identification of Best Practice : final report, national overview with individual project reports*, London: SWA Consulting for the DfEE.

Wood, A. (2000) *A Guide to Outreach with Laptops*, Leicester: NIACE.